TWENTY THREE FRAGMENTS OF MY YEAR

Vrinda Pandit

ISBN 978-93-5610-031-2
© Vrinda Pandit 2022
Published in India 2022 by Pencil

A brand of
One Point Six Technologies Pvt. Ltd.
123, Building J2, Shram Seva Premises,
Wadala Truck Terminal, Wadala (E)
Mumbai 400037, Maharashtra, INDIA
E connect@thepencilapp.com
W www.thepencilapp.com

Author biography

as humanly as it sounds — the about section did make me forget everything about myself yet here i am.

as much as i'm unsure about this impulse, i'm aware that i like being around words or jotting words down, so to say. will the 40-year-old me be proud of this 20 something as she tries her hand at what comes naturally to her? there's only one way to find out — a time machine, obviously.

i am from Lucknow, India, and am the daughter of a writer. i'm fortunate that my father's genes trickled down upon me and thus, here i am -- writing.

CONTENTS

Moments leading up to it...... 6

Of longing and musings...... 8

Father...... 10

A gentle arrival...... 11

A Giant Morose Bask...... 12

inner child...... 13

City!...... 16

Morning Commute...... 18

Friday noon...... 20

Hey, you!...... 22

July...... 25

Real Slim Shady couldn't stand up...... 28

A spiritual being...... 31

The sick affair...... 32

New Moon...... 33

December sun...... 35

Sombre is the night...... 37

To Buzz,...... 39

What truth seems like with Mary Jane...... 41

Law of One...... 42

Ma...... 43

Living with three senses 44

twenty ninth of December 49

Moments leading up to it

it's the way your father's cough reminds you of his dead brother.

the stagnation of letting your thoughts just pass you by.

or the stare into oblivion which fills your heart with sadness when you're surrounded with people.

being unproductive while trying to be the opposite.

to be.

calling it a block instead of laziness and lack of courage, thereof.

well framed thoughts of your fellow beings.

the post that made you feel full and insecure about it, at the same time.

the fleeting thought (read: person) that's been lingering for months.

words of encouragement – "it'll come by"

the therapy session that got shifted to next week.

the   attempt   to   catch   up   with   your
brother's humming singing

a million words of discouragement by your own self.

a friend leaving on a tuesday.

letting go and holding on

are you satisfied yet?

is everything externalized or the oblivious feeling persists?

too real or too sappy?

to be.

observation and perspective.

is it the end?

will it be the end if it still feels incomplete?

. . .

Of longing and musings

o, what are we if not for love, by love and of love

let's leave the constitution out of this affair

of mindful poetry to evade the corny-ness

of feeling them more than actually being with them

of defying every plausible logic as to how important they have become

ask my dream theatre - it can tell you the actuality without acting coy

of reaching a zero rhyme level

a state of frenzy now that i look back but

o, comfort was at the lack

of clearing the rhyme level now.

to hold and be held,

the important pleasures of life

of real musings, love and

of crummy sonnets that don't do justice to my thought

but if i felt any less, words wouldn't have fallen short

Father

my father is a writer and i've never finished reading his work.

no malice here, i say without a smirk.

there are days when i want to pick up one of his pieces and embrace it

but the nudge is never intense.

i don't talk to him about my love for writing and

one would think that that's dense

but that's how it is behind this fence.

how do i deal with the fact that the man whose genes made me a writer, isn't read by me?

how do i apologize to him for the decision that is consciously made by me?

A gentle arrival

i have a lot to feel but not the right words.

i want to write but with the right words.

i have been writing when grief arrives unexpectedly;

catches me off-guard; daily.

its arrival is as consistent as erraticity

time isn't the protagonist here - is a pity.

traipsing my way around as an attempt to not seem too melancholic

because grief leaving unexpectedly is also symbolic.

but who's to say when you're bowed -

and it gently sits across, looks you in the eye and stomps you to the ground.

A Giant Morose Bask

letting it envelop me

un-willing to sleep

in the p.m.

i repeat, un-willing

like, i'll miss out on feeling this feeling

this is very new to me

not the feeling - the unwillingness to dodge it

Cohen barges in with words that intensify the heavy-ness

a vain good attempt

should-could-would shut-eye

un-willing

shut-eye

inner child

i've been questioning myself for more than twenty-four hours now and i have to finish a few "educational quests" but i can't seem to concentrate so, here i am.

whoever reads this, i'd want to clarify that the lines written ahead don't portray hate for anyone mentioned – it's just my let-out.

i would've been ten or eleven years old when this happened – i used to go to these dance classes (in a school) near my home. although the distance could be covered on feet all alone, i wasn't allowed to do so; hence, my mother and brother accompanied me. the class hadn't started so we were all waiting outside the auditorium. my brother (eleven or twelve, then), who was going through a rebel phase in his life, wrote a cuss word on one of the doors of the school (with a marker) and also got caught eventually (lmao, very subtle of him).

as a result of gender biasedness or something that i don't know of, i fell prey to my mother's wrath and heard the words, "this wouldn't have happened if it wasn't for dropping you to your dance class" from her mouth.

a ten-year-old was subjected to these words from the person she listened to and looked up to the most, and things never remained the same because she actually believed it when her mother said that it was her fault.

an inner child was created and what creeped in, was a guilt conscience for the rest of my formative years. maybe that's why i apologize at the tip of my tongue and am so scared of messing up in all my relationships.

i dealt with this memory in therapy this year and unabashedly bawled my eyes out in front of my therapist. my brother knows about it too.

sometimes i wish i could tell ma about that day but i know i wouldn't hear the right words from her because she's dealing with her own issues and will only start questioning her parenting – which i don't want and which is why i resort to writing.

a few minutes back, a trivial issue at home led her to say to me that, "you're a very difficult child" when since the last twenty-four hours, i've been trying to tell myself that i'm not a mess-up and have been trying not to overthink every action of mine.

a third person might just get on with life without paying much heed to this but my inner child took it personally and so did i.

my emotionally aware self knew that if i don't deal with this now, I'll keep on replaying it in my head. i didn't want to believe her words this time so i texted my brother.

he told me that, "the only reason it will replay in your head is if you believe in it. you know who you are and no one can come and tell you otherwise – it'll only reside if you let it. you can heal the child by changing its beliefs or just imagine her inside you and sit with her – hold her hand and be the parent she deserves. tell her what you'd want to hear at that moment".

i did go on to parent and i think i was a good parent to myself. i wouldn't know for sure until a situation like this shows up again but i'm breathing better for now so wohoo to me

& young Vrin too, of course.

City!

the morning was hopeful.

one and a half journey – back and forth

forth is draining

occupied for feeling lost

like i don't belong, after all the parading.

my wiser self says it's overthinking;

me going back to old patterns

its credibility seems high

and maybe i am too lost in my sigh!

//

i never pictured myself writing in a metro

or at a station.

everyone seems to be occupied with their devices.

i do that too sometimes — the low look.

you detest the crowd and then you become it;

even if it is for a while.

how is it that i feel lost and still

hope that things might go uphill?

Morning Commute

it starts with a lot of self-doubt and ambiguity.

you're unsure about how patchy that road is and you trip
— almost trip

and hope that no one saw you.

you come off as timid and your stance alone portrays how
new you are here.

zoning out isn't a luxury you afford.

then comes the cribbing

not to forget how out of place you feel.

. . .

but now you're a part of the lot

and you know where the speed breakers are

you might even jump over it – at the beat of the current
track

you start to exude confidence and portray as though you
know the drill (even if you're a few days old there)

laid back posture –

staring into oblivion (a power pose, to say)

might even groove a bit – if the shuffle is an ally that day

zoning out and you reunite

only to realize that you missed your station;

again.

Friday noon

i have therapy at half-past three

booked a session after a crying spree.

i forgot what i was crying about,

it's been two months now.

/

i cribbed about the commute last Monday

i enjoy it now

who knew there'll come a day when I'll write around a crowd with devices and a bow.

/

i'm new to a city

i despised it

now, i'm observing it in its silence.

i'm looking at the places i might never visit

is this moment enough to manifest it?

i saw a lawn with luscious, ginormous trees,

i wonder how the noon there seems.

/

i see you in a lot of faces

i wonder what it'd be like if you weren't present just in phases.

you'd show me your cherished spot

and i'd look at you while you talk a lot.

/

i guess now would be a good time to jot down notes for my therapy appointment

. . .

Hey, you!

do you

listen to someone but suddenly realize that you weren't listening to them and then tell yourself to be present in the moment but keep oscillating back and forth in your head?

sleep early because the longing at night is too overpowering?

sometimes bask in that longing?

yearn for someone even during the day?

secretly want to be understood but are also scared of being understood?

suddenly feel so present in the moment that the sheer realness of the person in front of you comes as an overwhelming surprise?

feel like you can't take any more sorrow?

think you're still stuck in a particular month and haven't really moved on from there?

feel, on the good days, that you can conquer the world?

feel extremely shitty on the bad days and think that you'll never get through that day?

crack jokes to be liked?

look at yourself in the mirror daily, but still, forget what you actually look like?

love someone unconditionally?

just want to remain silent beside someone?

want to be hugged for an extra minute?

want to be parented in a better manner?

miss someone immensely and think about them in every breath you take?

think you can be kinder to yourself?

forgive the ones that hurt you?

forgive yourself?

feel a mammoth amount of love for your friends and just want to bask in their presence?

want human interaction but reach a saturation point immediately after?

miss someone's voice?

grieve with honesty when no one's around?

grieve unintentionally when you're surrounded by people?

joke around even when you feel like you're breaking from the inside?

do you feel free?

think your music taste is golden?

love yourself?

i know i do.

July

today, i noticed a waiter subtly prance along with the music after taking someone's order.

i crack lame jokes all the time.

i crack smart jokes when i'm comfortable around the people i'm with.

i interact with people but zone out very easily.

i try to make people laugh during these interactions.

most of the time, i'm just quiet – processing everything.

/

i smile randomly whilst thinking of someone.

i feel sorrow whilst thinking of the same person.

i dance to silly tunes in the shower.

i think about someone; have been; every day

/

i write when it feels right.

i listen to a lot of songs on loop.

my sleep breaks around 5 a.m. every day.

i haven't moved past the fifteenth minute of the tenth episode in the seventh season of Impractical Jokers, since Friday.

i'm on the fourteenth page of the history-genre book i'm trying to read for the first time.

i obsessively try to solve Sudoku.

/

i might have to skip a therapy session this month because i'm out of cash.

i ask people a lot of questions to get to know them better.

i'm fond of listening to their answers.

i like sitting on the grass.

i was startled when a man yelled on the road while i was driving.

/

i colored with my little cousins on a Thursday.

they taught me how to color outside the lines.

i made it a point to not correct them.

they're little monsters and i can't stand kids for long.

i hold my pen in a weird way.

/

sometimes, i hear myself breathe.

i try to be kind to everyone.

i weep.

i laugh easily.

/

i observe too much but sometimes, nothing at all.

i saw dadu dance with his hands (eyes closed) to the tunes of a song i can't recall.

today, i wrote.

Real Slim Shady couldn't stand up

you think you can handle something because you've been dealing with it for five years but then there comes a day when it slaps you on the face and you find yourself on the floor. quite literally.

in the latest episode of vrinpun's anxiety: she sat on the floor in order to ground herself, thinking the anxiety would kill her and mostly because, she didn't know what else to do.

{now that i continue to write about it, all of it seems redundant because i eventually got through it but it did really feel like the end of me and i did not think that i'd be able to make it. plus, everytime i'm going through an anxiety attack, i conveniently forget how bad the last one was. then i continue to dread the existing one because it seems worse, at the moment and also because i'm not really thinking straight. anxiety and memory loss go hand-in-hand, i suppose.}

so i sat on the floor with my 5th sudoku of the day, thinking that it'd help me distract myself. (i was wrong *wink face*)

i played my infamous "Bruh" playlist in the background for ultimate distraction.

Bruh – Numb by LP

V – um sure, Chester! i feel you. trust me, i do.

Bruh – Real Slim Shady by Eminem

Eminem – will the real slim shady please stand up

V – i mean, i would if i could?!?!? i can't really move here, so..

Eminem – your bum is on my lips, your bum is on my lips

V – breaks into a laugh while being on the verge of a helpless cry

shuts off Spotify

i switched to my DARE app (that i hadn't used in months) and clicked on the S.O.S button.

for the record: sudoku is still being solved…

my head – "you're going to die of this pain which feels like a heart attack/heart ache………………but oh, a 4 will come here and 2 will go there."

i swear i don't know how my brain did it but it did transition from a blackmailer to a sudoku solver within seconds.

so, then i tried to listen to the S.O.S. audio of this guy who comforted me by saying things like, "i'm with you" and "you won't die".

tries to breathe heavily and tries to internalise his words; whilst continuing to solve the sudoku

sudoku championship, here i come!!

it honestly bodes me well that i can write about the episode as a satire but this was the hardest thing i had to go through, in a while. i did eventually get up from the floor to fetch some water for myself and then went on to make fun of it on a blog.

but, imagine your chest hurting all day along with your tits; except you're not on your period and you can't even get a bypass.

stupid fucking anxiety, leave my tits alone!!!

A spiritual being

when you feel like you're an outlier here

a being from another tier.

when you feel like your physical body is getting lighter

a being without ego.

when you feel like love

like, there is only love, above.

you know that you carry a greater purpose;

when vibrations rise

and you let go of capsize.

when you see yourself in everyone

it's hard not to see everything as one.

The sick affair

i'm not very good at being sick

i crumble and sulk like an eight-year-old.

there's something so daunting and beautiful about this state

you don't have the energy to keep your guards up;

you're in your pure, vulnerable haste.

i fell sick last evening.

i wasn't on my best behavior

because i crumbled again in front of the mistress.

i wanted to rush to comfort but i couldn't

so i curled up and slept.

New Moon

several new moons have passed

and i have found myself looking up at night.

no one tells you that October brings with it a strange sense of release

which can make you feel lost and question things

because suffering can get comfortable.

and by the risk of sounding distraught, i say that

maybe the ones that leave, never really left and

i would explain it further but words might demean the feeling

so,

i hold back with a lot of feelings on standby.

i write this as my uterus bleeds and my stomach cramps up.

rest is due

but i wanted to bask in the daylight before twilight

so,

i came out to look up and around.

it got me thinking that

it's sacred how we tend to attach feelings to months or years.

maybe we're just latching it onto something trying to look for comfort because

comfort is all we seek

and maybe, just maybe,

seasons do carry that with them.

December sun

i had only heard of people telling time through the sun.

at twenty-three, i experienced it.

the room i stay in, faces the sun

thank you, windows

and lethargy

they led me to the unforgettable.

it starts on my left

i position myself diagonally and bask in it.

i would be lying if i say that i don't have the ulterior motive of staying warm.

i shift to the centre as it's twelve.

it starts to bother me,

a comfortable bother.

my insides feel grateful because moon time makes me whimper.

thank you, silence, delusion,

and music

they help me to stare at nothing.

it departs on my right

but today, i stepped out to see it off

and bask in it without any barriers.

Sombre is the night

i haven't written in a while

the last time i wrote, the breeze wasn't this cold.

i can guarantee that

winters, at some point in my life, will be the end of me

annually i'm reminded of how

i need to get used to bathing with warm water,

i just don't know how to.

different year, same story

i sulk about the season and continue to go on about my day, nonetheless.

i wore a sweatshirt today; it felt warmer

i got back home from an impulsive walk (to shoo the shiver away) and saw dadi.

dopamine made her witness my sashay

i sashayed some more beside her while she ate with an unimpressed face.

i gave up and sat down to eat with her

tough crowds are always a delight, you see

i sashayed more in my room;

sat down to write because i hadn't written in a while

. . . .

the night seems demure

dullsville weather

a burgundy sweatshirt

and half-worn blue socks

semi-warm hands fidgeting with the pen

because a clueless, yet occupied brain is forced to step up before ten.

To Buzz,

it's as if my past self doesn't want me to forget about this day.

as soon as i'm on the verge of not being aware of the 21st, i will suddenly get reminded of you.

i have grieved your death for years but now, i just feel extreme ecstasy at the thought of you.

i wish i was gen-z enough then, to capture you more

and i had the mind to understand you more.

but all i remember is your skin and eyes;

and i guess it's enough for me.

i have loved you at 11,

i love you even more at 23.

and i guess that's what separation leaves us with – a lot more love.

i remember hallucinating you even when i was sober.

my bedside still reeks of your presence,

and the balcony can still echo your bark.

i think everyone here misses you but i will let you on in the secret that i miss you the most.

hope you're happy,

i know i'm happy now, without you.

What truth seems like with Mary Jane

it makes you numb;

numb enough to feel.

static enough to stare at air consistently;

only to realize it's only been seconds.

it's liberating.

your heart feels your own

it asks you to nurture it,

to be it.

Law of One

let's let people be

let's see them as us.

a part of us;

that we might be rejecting.

let's accept us through us;

not from the outside

but from within.

let's see at last that

they are us.

Ma

ma (mother) has always liked dosa

i remember vividly how she delves into it

/

i grasped the smell of dosa today

and thought of ma

seemingly, my primal reaction to it.

/

i've never fancied a dosa;

the thought of ma nudged me to devour in it

/

i might tell others now

that i like dosa;

it reminds me of ma

Living with three senses

yes, i did have to ensure i was counting it right and i'm still very unsure so heheh *nervous laughter* hehehe.

it's the damnedest thing – eating without taste and not being able to smell even the lotion on your body – but it is what it is.

pro tip: first two days feel alien but humans get used to change and so did i.

pretty sure everyone is dealing with their own little battles but when they look around, they invalidate their own suffering and that's exactly what i did too after the fifth line.

raises hand for a virtual high five

humans don't ever fail to surprise me. everyone around me is attempting to do things to keep them sane/distracted – pick your choice.

binge-watching

cringe watching (guilty pleasures for the win)

meme consumption

re-watching YouTube videos

their stress levels are sky-rocketing but they still check up on each other without a second thought – ah, humanity isn't dead.

everyday dialogue between my friend and i:

"how're you?"

"how's everyone?"

"is the SpO2 level fine?"

"it's so hot"

"i need pizza"

(the last two statements is just me, obviously)

autocorrect is well versed with all of it by now.

another friend diligently calls me up daily to ask about my health – the consistency is uncanny.

health updates on one app, satisfactory memes on another – anything that might help another person is wonderful.

a few amalgamating source lists and sharing it across, others hoarding up on meme content to give others a laugh.

#covidheroeswearingcapes – thisissocringeykillmeplease

my friends try to come up with suggestions for me to watch.

my series-commitment-phobic ass neglects everything.

i turn to Keats followed by Piyush Mishra – is this coexistence even legal in one night? eh, whatever floats my boat.

dadu is an addition to the infected club. gets shifted upstairs in the room beside mine. an oxygen cylinder is also arranged for mayday.

he carries his radio with him.

Jagjit Singh sings in the background

Mishra distracts him and Keats stays with me.

my sibling has been asked to step foot in the city (an addition to manpower, i suppose).

dark humor companions will meet again.

humans losing humans.

friends losing family members.

my idea of being there for them: talk about how i coped with death in the past.

does it help? who knows. i was left on read.

grief is necessary and so is space – only wise to give it.

i learned this new term in therapy and it's called – "compassion fatigue".

PSA and further explanation: it's okay to look out for yourself even though you know that others are suffering and it's okay if you don't want to care about others too, for a change.

tries to shove the same PSA in her own functioning but fails miserably

father's lung infection takes a back seat at the thought of dadu getting infected. ah, the power of concern and love.

he'll probably suffer the consequences at night so good luck to him.

dadu did the same when he got to know about his son's suffering.

wow, these two!

why am i noticing all this? family dispute? where art thou?

anyway, Pandits can be weird and overwhelming so it's best to talk about the sanest one there – me, obviously.

stares awkwardly at the wall with curled lips whilst thinking about what to say

.

.

.

not being able to taste the food you're eating is positively correlated with the feeling of your stomach not being filled —– high chances that it's just me.

PSA to the 10% of people who actually read my word vomit:

meditation works wonders.

dancing while bathing is not good for your breath if you're infected – should've seen that coming.

prone breathing (lying on your stomach and breathing) helps — will create funny-looking marks on your body but that's okay. lift up your shirt, look at it, and put it back down —- that's what she said.

aha, humor is intact.

humor is the best defense mechanism out there – i do declare.

uncomfortable and unnecessary endnote – mother doesn't handle stress very well and it's been pretty interesting having her around…

sips water, gasps for air, breathes heavily, and vaguely stops writing

—— not dead ——-

twenty ninth of December

as i write on night twenty-one,

there's a lump in my throat

a lot of factors weigh in on this sinking boat.

i feel like a nomad who is fond of sitting alone

like the people around me give me their personality on loan.

i feel like there's not enough empathy within us;

not enough honesty;

just pretense adorned.

i yearn to spread kindness and love

'tis enough to get the world abuzz

/

i guess it's all i know

it's all i will ever know.

www.ingramcontent.com/pod-product-compliance
Lightning Source LLC
LaVergne TN
LVHW050425160726
843469LV00041B/1238